THE INSIDER'S GUIDE

TO WHERE AND HOW TO BUY A CAR

Strike a Deal at the Dealership

JOE DIFEO

CHAPTER ONE

ALL IN THE FAMILY

ARE YOU DREADING your next car purchase? Would you rather go to the dentist than start your next car search? Car buying doesn't have to painful…and let me explain why.

So, you're thinking about buying a car. You probably already have the car in mind: the make; the model; new or used; if it's used, the desired miles; maybe even the color. You may even have a few dealerships you are considering, either because you have heard about them by word of mouth or from those annoying advertisements where they seem to always be yelling and screaming at you, offering these "unbelievable" savings that you MUST take advantage of NOW!

Like any customer, you want a good car and a fair deal. A dealership seems like the best way to go. But how do you know if you're choosing the right one? How do you make sure you get a fair deal? Are all dealerships to be trusted equally?

This guide is structured to provide you with an ideal game plan for this important undertaking to ensure that you get the best value for your budget by following a series of simple but crucial steps. By the time you turn the final page, you'll know how to pick a great dealership, what to do when you get there, and how to get the car you want at a fair price.

How do I know this? My family has been running dealerships up and down the east coast for decades. In this book, I'm going to give you the insider's knowledge you always wanted but were either too anxious to ask or simply didn't consider. I'm a current dealership owner, and car dealerships have been in my family for three generations. From the perspective of a dealership owner, the better informed our customers are, the better the chance that they will not only be pleased with the value of their purchase but will find it such a rewarding experience they come back when it's time for the family to purchase another car. That's how my family has thrived in this business, by making sure folks like you become lifetime customers who share their experience with friends and family. Building lasting extraordinary relationships has and always will be good business.

My family's venture into the business began with my great-great grandfather, Saverio DiFeo, who migrated from Italy with his family in the early 1900s. He got his start in the New World peddling fruits on the streets of Little Italy in New York City. Like many immigrants to this country he was motivated to create a good life for his family – building a foundation for the success of future generations.

Eventually, his son Joseph moved to Jersey City and opened a bakery, DiFeo's Pastry Shop, in the Italian ghetto, where he and his family lived in the floors above the bakery. The bakery was nothing very fancy, but it was good, and word of mouth spread in the community, as always happens when an outstanding product is delivered at a good price with care for the customer.

In those days, much like today, word of mouth was everything. You couldn't afford to have dissatisfied customers. The bakery was filled with the best pastries in town, and My grandfather Sam worked there, learning the focus on customer service and satisfaction he would one day bring to his own business ...and that's where the cars come in.

By the late 1940s, looking to strike out on his own, Sam partnered with a friend, Frank, and opened his first used car dealership on Newark Avenue. At the time, he didn't know a thing about cars, but he knew people. He also knew the secrets to keeping customers so satisfied that when it came time for them to choose a place to spend their hard-earned dollars there was no use risking it with someone who didn't consider you a part of the family.

I imagine customers felt as comfortable around Sam as all fourteen of us grandchildren did when we'd congregate at his house. Sam and his wife had four children—my dad Joseph, my Uncle Sam, my uncle Dennis, and my aunt Cecilia. You'd think the owner of a big car dealership would be taking his grandchildren for spins around the block in the latest model, but instead we usually enjoyed his homemade strawberry shortcake with whipped cream made from scratch. Even more enticing was his lemon ice maker—this big wooden barrel that you'd have to crank, crank, crank with the salt and ice and eventually be rewarded with the most delicious cold Italian lemon ice in all of Jersey. That was the magic of my grandfather Sam—he made you feel like you were important, at ease, like you *mattered*.

No doubt he practiced this with every customer that walked through the doors of his dealership also. Sam DiFeo wasn't just about selling great cars at a great value, he was about helping people and making them smile.

Sam brought the lessons he learned at the pastry shop—that community is everything, that word of mouth is invaluable, and that the customer is always right—and applied them to his dealership. Frank often drove the cars from the lot over to the bakery and there they'd appraise them while enjoying a tasty treat. Plus, Sam was a "yes man." If a customer had a complaint, he was sure to make it right. Simply, he cared about his customers. They were, after all, his neighbors in the community and he took that very seriously.

Eventually, a manufacturer called Willys-Overland Motors approached them. Willys-Overland was an American company best known for its design and production of military Jeeps and the civilian versions of the same. Soon after, the dealership was rebranded with the Willys-Overland Motors name, and business boomed. Sam and Frank opened their second location, a Plymouth dealership, in nearby Linden, New Jersey. Shortly after, in 1953, they opened a Buick dealership.

When my dad, Joe Sr., graduated from Boston College in 1965, he went on to law school and soon after began practicing law. He also started helping with the family business on the side, mostly with legal matters. But by the early 1970s he'd made the transition, and started working in the car business full time. His brother, my Uncle Sam, wasted no time and started working in the business right after graduation. Not long after my dad started working full time in the car business with them, Toyota approached the two brothers.

Toyota was really taking off—it was the seventies and the company was actively looking to expand into new markets. It was seeking to do business with established dealership owners with solid reputations. That's how the fourth location came to be. My dad and uncle bought a gas station and converted it into the new Toyota franchise.

As if that wasn't enough, my grandfather had always dreamed of owning a Cadillac dealership. With enough capital and experience under his belt, he opened a Cadillac dealership in the late seventies. While the Plymouth and Willy's Overland dealerships had been shuttered, the family now had four thriving locations: Pontiac, Buick, Toyota, and Cadillac.

By the end of the eighties, four original stores had turned into thirty-five stores, and cars were the official DiFeo family business. Though they expanded rapidly, they made sure each store operated with the same rules and procedures as the initial stores. Again, it always went back to concern and care for the customer and firm roots in the community.

Eventually, Wall Street came knocking. Looking for an established string of close-proximity dealerships with a clean brand and impeccable reputation, United Automotive went public in the nineties, eventually becoming Penske Automotive. The family eventually sold twenty-five dealerships, and kept ten.

It's hard to say what contributed specifically to such astonishing success. Of course, a lot of hard work and dedication no doubt proved crucial factors. But other owners worked just as long hours with similar devotion and failed to reach such stellar results over the years. So, it had to be more than just that.

Our family did things a little differently than dealerships had done in the past. Like in the bakery, once the quality of the goods reached a superior level, the focus widened to superior customer service. We made up a survey for customers, for example, and asked them when they would most like their car serviced. More than half of those surveyed chose Saturday. Up to that point, no dealership service departments were open Saturdays. Our family dealerships found a way to make it happen and how to make it appealing for the mechanics and other staff as well. After all, if you're going to be a customer-focused business, it's imperative that you listen to what the customer is saying. We believed in giving customers what they wanted. We also established a two-week return policy. It was a different way of looking at things—we viewed everything in the business from the customer's perspective.

Customers, indeed the entire city, eventually responded to such unprecedented attention and service. Jersey City even recognized my grandfather as an extraordinary citizen and named a street, Sam DiFeo Drive, after him.

You may have noticed that this story features five generations of DiFeos from my great-great grandfather to my father, and you may wonder where I come in and how I earned my insider credentials as your guide. I'm afraid I was, for a period, the black sheep of the family. Despite all my family's success and my years' experience working after school and weekends at dealerships most of my life, after I graduated from college I did what any son of a dealership legacy would do...I moved to Asheville, North Carolina, and opened an organic farm.

My life was the typical existence of a small farmer: early mornings, seven days a week, hard work, and quiet, lots of quiet, except for the roaring of tractors now and then. Although I loved working with the soil and producing outstanding fruits and vegetables for the community, the isolation, long hours, and meager profits eventually began taking their toll.

My friends encouraged me to join the family business, but I still wasn't convinced the car business was for me. Rather than scrap everything, I found a sales job at a local dealership to feel the business out as a regular Joe and see how I'd do.

I did exceedingly well, making top salesman right out of the gate. After a year and a half, I met someone on a similar trajectory (does this story sound familiar?), and we joined forces, partnering to open a used car dealership. I was walking in Sam DiFeo's footsteps, in a new city, on my own. We even branded the dealership (ours was a Thrifty Car Sales location) the way my grandfather had with Willys-Overland so many years before. Like my grandfather, as owners we made sure the focus remained on the customer, making it a point to help many credit-challenged folks get a good car. We always focused on getting quality cars and selling them at a fair price to make sure that our customers drove away in a car they could trust and not feeling as if they had been financially hobbled.

Our focus wasn't just on selling cars to people, it was on helping people find solutions and improving their credit and transportation situations. Like the men in my family before me, I strongly believe that good business is founded on relationships, not transactions. The dealership did well, and one day, a gorgeous girl came in looking to buy a car. After the sale, I knew right away I was interested in seeing this customer again very soon. Eventually we got married and continued to live in Asheville running that dealership until another opportunity came along.

My family had a Volkswagen dealership in New Jersey for decades, and Volkswagen invited them to open another one in Florida. In 2011, my family invited me to join my brother Andrew in St. Augustine, Florida, where he ran a successful Hyundai dealership he had opened a few years before. I jumped at the opportunity and my wife and I— expecting twins at the time—packed up and moved to St. Augustine.

I helped my brother expand the used car section of the Hyundai store while we built the Volkswagen dealership across the street. We opened VW for business just before Christmas in 2013. Santa—well, the VW factory—delivered about 100 shiny new VW's to fill up the blacktop. With our purpose of "Driving Extra-Ordinary Relationships," we focused on making purchasing and servicing a high-value and positive experience for our guests.

That's the kind of experience I want for you and any customer, particularly those with concerns and hesitations based on lack of available information or unsatisfactory experiences in the past. That's the main purpose of this book. By guiding you through the process, educating you on factors that directly affect your choices, and dispelling myths and misconceptions, this book seeks to empower you as a buyer by giving you the tools and resources to find the highest quality car for the best value.

Everyone buys cars, but most people dread the process because they fear it unfolds as if in a foreign land where they do not speak the language. In THE INSIDER'S GUIDE TO WHERE AND HOW TO BUY A CAR, I want to provide you with a resource that will help you choose the right dealer, select the right car, ensure the best price, and seal the deal by securing the best terms for payment.

I want you to feel like you can walk into a showroom confident you'll be treated with fairness and honesty. I want you to be secure in the fact that by choosing a reputable dealer and asking the right questions, the car buying process can be an enjoyable experience.

If I can achieve that for you going in, most likely you can drive off with confidence in your decision. That is, you can drive off happy and remain satisfied enough with the dealership post-sales and through the service life of the car to become a lifetime customer, part of the dealership's extended family.

CHAPTER TWO:

ACKNOWLEDGING THE PROBLEM

WALK INTO ANY DEALERSHIP on any given day and you might hear a conversation just like this:

> *Salesman: Anyway, let's get serious, you wanna buy this car or not, yay or nay?*
>
> *Customer: Well I don't know, we have to think about it.*
>
> *Salesman: What's there to think about? You told me you like it, you asked me ten thousand questions, I answered every single one of them, you drove it, you love it, what more do you need to know?*

The salesman is aggressive, pushy, with a "typical" car salesman attitude, right? Well, this dialogue is from the script for the 2002 Robert De Niro movie *Analyze That* in which he played the classic, clichéd example of the kind of salesman every car-buying customer has come to dread. Sure, it was an exaggeration for comic effect, but clichés don't spring from out of nowhere. They come bubbling up from the grain of truth—that's why we recognize them.

So, is the cliché of the pushy, aggressive car salesman true? Or is it just an outdated fear? It's true that somewhere there is probably a guy just like De Niro's character, but that guy is the exception to the rule.

A recent survey measured consumer trust of dealer salespeople, and the results were humbling for car professionals everywhere: only 21 percent claimed they perceive them as "trustworthy"— lower on the totem pole of trust than lawyers, mortgage brokers, or insurance brokers. Worse, 56 percent of consumers rated car salespeople untrustworthy. Dealerships have a serious problem: and it is one of perception and image of the hardworking employees that staff them.

What it all comes down to is that if you're in the market to buy a car you might have a certain degree of fear. Fear that your salesman might not have your best interest at heart. Fear of the complexities of financing. Fear of not getting a good deal. Fear of getting stuck with a lemon. What you don't realize is that the salesman fears that you are seeing him through those clichéd lenses, as someone who isn't honest or sincere. Car salespeople are constantly working against that stereotype. They also must deal with the pressures of any type of salespersons; they must convince customers day in and day out that what they are offering is the best quality for the best value. As a dealership owner, there are ways to make the salesperson's job less strenuous such as providing them with a quality product to sell, and creating a culture of customer service and transparency.

So, there's fear from both sides. The fact of the matter is that purchasing a vehicle is the second biggest purchase you will ever make. A little fear and anxiety is natural. This chapter will help you cut through any excess fears and misapprehensions by laying out the facts.

There has been an undeniable amount of change in the industry that can put your fears to rest. Consider where we started and how far we've come. The way business was done prior to the advent of the Monroney Sticker in the 50's has really stuck in people's minds, although the sticker itself ushered in a whole new era of car buying with protections for the consumer firmly in place. In the past, when dealers arranged financing, they used to be able to charge whatever interest rate they wanted. Thus, this led to some dealers wildly profiting from unfair rates above those charged by the lender. With more regulation across the entire finance industry, such abuses have been curtailed dramatically: now the lender controls the terms of the loan and it is based on the credit of the individual.

So, what is the Monroney Sticker? In 1955, the Senate established the Interstate and Foreign Commerce Committee, charged with overseeing the automobile marketing practices subcommittee. This was in direct response to dealer complaints of dishonest actions by automakers, particularly in the awarding of franchises. Senator Mike Monroney, the subcommittee's chairman, was essential in passing the Automobile Dealers' Day in Court Act in 1956, which provided some recourse for dealers with complaints against manufacturers. I know what you're thinking—what does this have to do with dealers ripping people off?

Once the subcommittee delved into the auto manufacturers' practices, they also uncovered widespread questionable dealer practices. After the hearings ended in 1958, Senator Monroney drafted the price-sticker bill. Before both houses passed the bill, the National Automobile Dealers Association and the Detroit automakers endorsed it. The bill was signed into law in July of 1956. Prior to this legislation, there was no resource whatsoever for the consumer to know what the manufacturer suggested retail price of a vehicle should be. Once the law was enacted all vehicles had to display the sticker on a window, which could only be removed by the customer after purchase. Before this, dealers could play consumer ignorance and price cars at whatever amount they wanted—and they too often did. But like any other industry, the car business has changed.

But something to keep in mind is that even though the industry is more regulated, most dealerships are not corporations—they are privately owned and run, so the customer experience has a wide range of variations. That's why it is important to find the right dealer, one with your interest in mind. And because you are a representative of the larger community when you walk through the doors of a dealership, among the two most important characteristics of a top-notch dealership are that it is locally owned and fully invested in the community.

Another thing that's changed over the years is the amount of information available to the consumer. Access to information has increased dramatically with the explosion of resources available on the Internet. In recent years, consumer guides like the Kelly Blue Book have begun to publish and update their data online without requiring a subscription. Most dealerships have their pricing for new and used cars on their own website, and such information is also featured in third-party sites like Autotrader and Cars.com. Changes over the past ten years have also enabled customers to get vehicle specs and options and pricing information from multiple online guides, manufacturer sites, and third-party sites; value their trade in; compare cars on multiple dealers' lots; and get financing information. They can even get approved for financing online.

What do all these research resources mean for dealerships? Fewer visits to the lot, without a doubt. On average, car buyers visit 1.2 dealerships before making a purchase, down from over five on average a decade ago. Instead of visit to the brick and mortar shop, consumers visit ten online sites on average now before making a purchase. It makes sense then, that by the time they're ready to buy, they're very likely to only visit one or two lots.

So how much research do you need to do? The average research timeline for a new car purchase is four months, but that includes the casual browsing when the buyer initially starts thinking about getting a new car. Studies show that once a customer has made a definitive decision to purchase, that research timeline shrinks to one week.

This busy online week is when you as an educated consumer get the answers to all the questions you might have relied on the salesman to answer in the past. You might want to know which car is safer, which seats five vs. seven (with gear in tow), what the lowest monthly payment might be on the car of your dreams, or what kind of extras you can get on a desired model. All these answers are now just a Google search away. Having such information before choosing a dealership is also one of the best ways for you to reduce your fear and anxiety going in.

Research equals power.

And once you have all your questions answered, you go to the lot and test-drive the car you're interested in, right?

Not always.

A recent survey of 2,000 automotive consumers found that 16 percent never test-drove the vehicle prior to purchase, while 33 percent test-drove only one car before purchasing. On average, car buyers test-drive only 1.9 cars, with about 26 percent test-driving 3 vehicles or more. Whether you're a test-driver or not, going in armed with the information you've researched online is a sure-fire way to be able to communicate to the salesperson exactly what you want and are flexible about, so you can work as a team to make sure you get the highest quality at the best value of your choice.

Not all the research happens at the outset, either. Once you've decided on a car, if you're buying a used car, the vehicle history report— Carfax being the most well-known and readily available— arms you with more knowledge. Vehicle history reports, or VHRs, are like the biography of the vehicle, including accidents, red flag indicators such as flood, salvage, or frame damage; the number of owners, and the maintenance history. You can purchase a vehicle history report online, but most dealers (who typically pay a flat fee for unlimited reports at their own expense as a service to the customer) will and should provide one for you on any pre-owned vehicle you consider.

Buying a car is a huge investment with a big price tag, second in value commonly only to your home. In many other industries, there is a huge markup in price—furniture and mattresses, diamonds, designer handbags, and other luxury goods are all sold for much more than the amount for which they are purchased wholesale or the cost to manufacture them. Therefore, if you're like most car buyers, you probably assume cars have an enormous markup too. This is an understandable misconception but one that also fuels the stereotype about swindling car salespersons and underhanded dealership practices.

Per a TrueCar-commissioned survey, consumers believe car dealers make about five times more profit on the sale of a new car than they do. That's right. Car buyers believe dealerships make five times the profit they make. That one statistic alone may be enough to explain the trust gap and the fear factor at play in the relationship between consumers and dealers.

The main fear you have is this: that you'll overpay. You, like most, believe dealers make around a 30 percent profit on the sale of a $30,000 car. The reality is something much different. Per the research from the National Automobile Dealers Association, profits on new-car sales have fallen dramatically: from 5.5 percent in 2003 to 3.8 percent in 2013.

Three-point-eight percent.

The same study laid bare the reality that fear and mistrust have had very negative consequences for both consumers and dealers in the car-buying process. The truth is, if consumers believe they are getting trustworthy information through a transparent process, they're more likely to feel less fear, less stress, and a sense of ease that they've made a transaction that is fair and sound.

Doing your research before you buy is one way to work toward that goal. Moreover, knowing unequivocally that the margin of profit is not the astronomical amount you might have assumed; in fact, it is trending at the other end of the spectrum, should assuage your fear of being overcharged and make you understand that there is only so much wiggle room for any dealership when it comes to negotiating sticker price. Armed with knowledge, you'll be able to purchase your new vehicle with confidence and, with any luck, a little bit of joy.

Now that you know what to look for in a car, and the kind of research you should do before you even choose a dealership, you'll need to know what to look for in a dealership.

CHAPTER THREE

DEALERSHIP 101

BEFORE YOU WALK INTO A DEALERSHIP, you should know a little bit about the nature of the business to avoid taking detours that will prolong and dampen the experience. Purchasing a car is a major life decision, like applying to college or moving to a new town. You should never begin such a journey without some preliminary knowledge of the terrain.

So, let's begin with some simple facts about which there may be some misconceptions. Except for a few showcase stores in New York and other mega-cities, manufacturers don't own dealerships. A recent exception to this is the Tesla brand which owns all its showrooms.

Independent entities own and operate all other dealerships in the United States. A very small portion of these owners are publicly owned companies (listed on the stock exchanges). Some of these dealer groups are very large, such as AutoNation, the largest volume seller of new cars in the United States. Although public dealer groups have continued to expand and open new dealerships, they own only about 5 percent of all the dealerships in the country. CarMax is the only publicly traded used car dealership.

Most dealerships are privately owned. They're owned by individuals or families that most often reside in the community that the dealerships are located. In that sense, these dealerships are no different than my grandfather's first dealership on Newark Avenue in Jersey City or my first dealership in Asheville, North Carolina. Like my grandfather and me, these private owners are likely not strangers to the secret that the best way to thrive in any business is to put the people that you want to attract into the dealership first. And that means you, the customer.

Every dealership has different approaches to doing business and serving customers. So, before I extol the virtues of privately owned dealerships, and there are many such virtues, you should be warned that if you ever visit more than a few, you may grow frustrated by the slight adjustments you'll have to make as customer in the way you interact with salespersons, the way you approach the final crucial steps before committing to a purchase, and the process of securing financing. No two privately owned dealerships are run in the same manner. Even dealerships associated with the same manufacturer often have very different approaches to making the customer experience fulfilling in such a way as to retain the customer for a lifetime of car purchases.

When I opened my first dealership, there were some strategies and objectives that I shared with those of my grandfather Sam DiFeo and every other dealership owner in my family line: great cars at great values, making every potential buyer who walked through the door feel as if they mattered just as much as the buyer in the final steps of the process, establishing roots in the community through building customer trust, and cultivating relationships beyond the customer base.

I saw a need that wasn't being served fully in this community as well. People with challenged credit had limited options in purchasing quality cars. Small buy-here pay-here operations would finance them but usually only offered high-mileage cars prone to quickly need repairs. New car stores could sometimes arrange financing but would often not have the proper staff, expertise or specialized banking relationships to help. By focusing on keeping the right late model cars in inventory and developing relationships with the right lenders we provided an alternative to the folks with challenged credit. They could purchase and finance a reliable car and at the same time improve their credit ratings with timely payments.

My grandfather and I travelled different roads toward the same destination. The strength of both our approaches lay in understanding the community we served. Yet, you could go to two dealerships of the same manufacturer a mere thirty miles apart and have very different experiences, depending on owner philosophy and customer history. Car dealership franchises do not adhere to the strict standardization regulations of other type of franchises, such as those of McDonald's, for example.

Such variance should not alienate you when you visit dealerships, although it may stir anxiety in a process that many already experience as too intimidating. Consistency allows corporate dealerships to quickly instill confidence in the customer through familiarity. This is true of any type of corporate franchise. No matter where in the country you walk into an Apple store, interactions with salespeople, the products, and the way they are displayed remain mostly consistent. However, consistency may not always be beneficial if the familiar feeling the customer experiences when walking into a corporate chain store is one of lack of connectedness or of anonymity.

The good news is that many privately-owned dealerships understand the value of putting the customer's needs first. They contribute to the growth and development of the community not only in the economic sphere, but also by creating trusting bonds with their customers that reverberate beyond the car business. These dealerships practice the resolution of issues in a personal way, and are often highly visible in the community through service and monetary support.

At a local dealership, you will find someone who will sit down with you to solve a problem, whether such an issue arises in the process of buying car or after you have driven out of the lot. Because these dealerships can set their own operating frameworks, they have the flexibility to "go beyond the rules." Instead of corporate "no return" policies, the local dealership is there to help solve your problem, work things out, and continue to build on the trust channels that were opened the moment you first walked through the doors. Or as we shall see, even before that, when you first landed on the dealership's website.

So how do you find a local dealership that stakes its growth, development, and survival on functioning precisely this way?

In today's world, the face of a dealership from the customer's perspective may have less to do with its showroom windows than by how the dealership represents itself online. This is where most customers today have their first interaction with a dealership, during the initial period when they begin exploring options, doing research, and planning the next stage on the Internet.

You can get a sense of the culture of a dealership, the philosophy of its ownership, and its relationship to the community and its customers from its website and social media pages. Is the design and content of the dealership's website geared toward informing you and setting the groundwork for long-lasting mutually beneficial relationship? Or are the home pages so heavy on the sales mantras that the relationship with the customer is limited to a financial transaction?

Get a sense of the visual and verbal messages that the pages of these sites portray by imagining their impact if the same style and tone were replicated in a bricks-and-mortar dealership. A site with an overbearing or hardcore sales pitch, link after link, reveals the priorities and principles of the dealership. You would be naïve to believe that the tone changes once you walk through doors of the actual dealership.

Most dealership websites know that it takes more than a blaring sales pitch worthy of a late-night infomercial barker to engage and retain the attention today's info-savvy car buyer. Thus, after the initial impression of a website to gauge the most obvious aspects of a dealership's culture, you should continue with a more nuanced and detailed approach to evaluate the customer's place in it.

Is the website customer-centric and easy to navigate? Telephone numbers and email and street addresses should be listed on the home page or through a contact link that is easy to find. Customers often go to a website solely for this information.

Social media links should also appear on the home page. A map function with directions also helps customers get a sense of the location when planning visits to several dealerships. Subject links should include main topics such as Inventory, Financing, and an About Us section that gives customer a summary of the advantages of using the dealership.

Content in each of the categories should answer many of the questions you have about the process and car options. If it doesn't, then it's likely that the content may not be written with the customer fully in mind, a red flag. If a dealership spends no time and effort to include photographs of the actual cars available, and stock photos have been inserted, what does that say about how much time a dealership is willing to devote to you in person? Most dealerships employ best practices in their operating structure. This is one of the things consumers demand most, along with extensive and specific information on the models and makes they are considering.

Along with real-model updated photos, the pricing needs to be apparent in the inventory section. Is the lack of pricing information used as lure to call the dealership? What would you think of a relationship with another person that began with such purposeful tricks? Would you pursue it? Respond in kind to a dealership that uses such tactics. If all it says is "contact us," that's a red flag.

The manufacturer's suggested retail price and the sale price should be clearly readable for every model. Cars on the website should also be in stock. Whether the consumer feels misled on purpose or by mistake, the consequence is similar. The trust foundation becomes wobbly.

Do the owners show up prominently on any of the website's pages? Or are they to busy appearing in TV commercials, but inaccessible to the customer, as if owners run the show best behind some curtain. Even the President of the United States accepts emails. He is much busier, right? I laugh at the thought of my grandfather Sam

DiFeo telling his staff that they weren't allowed to let people contact him.

Prominent bios of managers and other personnel in the "About Us" or "Meet Our Staff" sections allow potential buyers to explore the human element of the place, without which the dealership would just be a very fancy parking lot. Is staff simply listed without direct contact info? Are staff pictures provided? The fewer items of information on such pages, the greater the likelihood the dealership may have a revolving door. Trust wavers when repeat buyers must introduce themselves to new salespeople.

Category links to areas of engagement outside the dealership boundaries, such as a link for "In the Community," tacitly express connections that inspire trust in the buyer. What level of involvement does the dealership have in your community?

From here, follow the links on the websites to the dealership's sites on social media. The evaluation of these sites should be like that of the main website, moving from broad, general, and initial impressions to more focused analyses of the types of posts and dealership reviews. Are the posts mostly sales pitches? Do they provide links to articles geared toward educating the consumer and improving service? Are there posts acknowledging team members' accomplishments (inside and outside of work), a sign that the dealership considers its personnel people as much as employees.

Engagement from visitors in the form of comments, likes, reviews, shares, or retweets provide evidence of virtual activity, which for at least some segments of the population equate with real-life buzz. Inactive or lazily managed social media sites suggest that customers have little loyalty or that marketing strategies need to be rescued from the Middle Ages.

Does the dealership respond and engage on the sites? Are responses canned? If so, such sites may pretend to be about customer engagement, but are simply well-disguised sales pitches. Many major dealerships outsource control of social media sites to professionals that specialize in social media stagecraft that provides the sheen of authenticity. It doesn't take long for the savvy consumer to notice, and not much longer to grow suspicious about, where else such a sheen plays a deceptive role in the dealership or its products.

When searching for review sites, it should be noted that there is valuable information to be mined in almost all of them. Google provides the largest number of reviews, mostly with a realistic balance that sheds light on the positive and negative qualities of a dealership. The algorithms in Google's also are set to filter out fake entries.

Sites with a small number of samples do not allow you to make an informed evaluation. If only negative or only positive reviews appear on a site, consider the likelihood of such one-sided interactions with customers in any type of business. Some sites don't even try to disguise the exaggeratedly stellar reviews, such as shopping sites like Cars.com and Edmunds, which actively encourage visitors to write exuberant reviews.

In general, consider the overall rating first, such as the average number of stars out of five. The more reviews included in the average, the more trustworthy the evaluation. Just as important if not more so than the average rating is how a dealership responds to negative reviews. Businesses are run by human beings. Everyone makes mistakes, even very skilled personnel with important responsibilities. When the results of such actions affect customers, issues come up, and a dealership betrays its nature most clearly in how such issues handled.

What should you look for in the response?

1. Acknowledgement of the customer's feelings on the issue.

2. A candid apology.

3. Desire to come to a more satisfactory resolution, with a specific invitation to reach out.

In cases in which the dealership is not to blame, does the tone remain conciliatory? Even if the customer is wrong—that is the perspective: "there's no arguing a perspective." Avoid dealerships whose responses need to one-up customer complaints with subtly condescending tone or content.

Choose a few dealerships with which to conduct online or real-life initial interactions, by:

1. submitting an information request,

2. calling, or

3. arranging a visit to the dealership

During your visit, staff and salespeople should be prompt and personable while maintaining a professional demeanor. Sales staff, service personnel, and financial managers should address your questions in a direct manner without veering from the subject, and elaborating upon the matter on request. Rambling or non-sequitur responses imply lack of knowledge. Your primary questions should all be addressed without obfuscation or misdirection.

After you have left the dealership, does the salesperson follow up in a low-pressure fashion? You should not feel as if you need to strategize an opportunity to hang up when engaged in such a call. Follow-ups that include a continuation of the previous conversation express interest in guiding the consumer to a satisfied purchase. Such actions become self-defeating if the customer feels harassed or pressured. A professional stays on top of things and leaves you with the impression they have taken over part of your research and lent you their experience and skills.

As you can see, there are many elements that go into making a customer's experience a success even before a decision to purchase becomes imminent. No dealership is perfect, but the best dealerships encourage potential customers to become even better informed....and that is what you should want.

All these factors impact the various stages of a purchase, and depending on the buyer and the circumstances and needs, some factors may be more prioritized in the decision process regarding what dealerships to visit.

Customers value time. Attempting to divert them to score a sale robs them of any time saved before the visit. Such short-term perception of what a customer represents devalues the interaction between seller and buyer and does more to reanimate the myth of the "typical" car salesman than a grand performance by even a genius like De Niro.

Instead of diverting them, a successful salesperson acts more as a guide and partner, making customers feel more empowered than when they first walked in, fully informing them of options such as leasing and financing differences that only very knowledgeable customers are fully informed about. Such options open the field for a customer and can widen the range of choices considerably as covered in the following chapter.

CHAPTER FOUR:

FINANCING, LEASING, AND CREDIT

ONE OF THE MOST IMPORTANT FACTORS to consider in purchasing your vehicle is financing. If you're thinking about financing through your chosen dealer, you are in good company. Most buyers finance their car purchases through dealerships. Fewer than 20 percent of buyers don't use the dealership financing. However, all possibilities should be considered at first in search for the best deal.

Because, as with buying a home, purchasing a car is such a big-money purchase, you are more than likely going to be financing. About 20 percent of buyers pay cash, but not everyone has that luxury, so financing becomes a necessary step in the process. The most common concerns customers have regarding the ins and outs of financing is their set budget. That is, is the monthly payment going to be reasonable? To properly address that question as a consumer, you need to consider three crucial factors:

1. the amount financed,

2. the term of the loan, and

3. the rate of the loan.

The average term for a loan to purchase a new car is about sixty-six months or five and a half years. If you put a significant amount as a down payment, the interest rate will be better. As a rule, however, you should not get too caught up on rate differences because with auto financing such differences are not going make a significant overall difference. Why? Because while a .5 percent rate difference would lead to significant amount in a house purchase, it will not make a large impact on a $25,000 car loan over the course of six years.

There are several major advantages to dealership financing. Most importantly, dealerships typically have relationships with ten to twenty different lenders, some with which they may conduct a high volume of business. Some of the perks offered in return for such volume are much lower rates for all different kinds of loans than a single individual could qualify for at the same bank. The volume relationship between dealership and lender is, in effect, a major advantage to the consumer and one of the reasons most financing is done through the dealership.

Another advantage of in-house financing stems from the long-held relationships dealerships have cultivated with multiple banks, so they can easily shop around for the best terms for you.

You may be concerned that multiple credit inquiries might negatively affect your credit score. This, however, is not the case in such instances. Though at one time it may have, the credit bureaus Equifax, Experian, and Transunion have adjusted their scoring model so that an auto loan inquiry from different banks *within a two-week period* counts as one inquiry. It is understandable that people will shop around, therefore the change in policy with the credit bureaus. Now if you are continually looking for credit over a longer period, such events will negatively affect your score. It's best to be prepared and not make multiple inquires until you're ready to buy.

Another factor to consider is that most dealerships have relationships with institutions that offer special programs for unique situations.

If your credit rating is challenged, some opportunities exist. Sometimes the only (and best) hope for financing a car with bad credit is through the dealership. Some of these lenders do not even do business directly with consumers, working only with dealerships instead. These kinds of lenders will take loans with consumers that would not qualify for a loan at a bank.

This is what's called "subprime credit". "Damaged credit" is a more proper way to phrase it. By whatever name, there is hope for even those with the most negative credit history. These lenders will look more closely at the situation and the specifics of your credit challenges when making their decision to fund.

Now, you're probably thinking, *will such a loan be an okay deal?* If you're someone that already has credit problems, the last thing you want is a bad deal. Yes, your interest rate might not be as good as someone with pristine credit, but there is something positive that can come out of it, aside from the car you drive out of the lot. Getting a loan on your vehicle is an opportunity to rebuild your credit. Every month you pay that note on time, your credit score will be positively affected. Over time, this can significantly impact your credit score in a positive way. The high interest rate may feel painful, but it affords you a chance to rebuild your credit and reflects—on the lender's part—the high risk the lender is taking with you.

Maybe your problem isn't bad credit but no credit at all. There are also first-time buyer programs through dealerships that aren't available to the public for people with no credit at all. This can be the first chance to obtain and start building a favorable credit history.

The other thing that consumers can't get anywhere else is that the dealership can get you captive financing. "Captive financing" is another name for credit offered by a company that is a subsidiary of the manufacturer. Volkswagen has VW Credit, for example. All major vehicle manufacturers have some form of captive financing available. The manufacturer subsidizes these financing companies so that they can sell more cars. These companies often offer below market rates, sometimes even zero percent. There can be a trade off with taking those below market rates, however. Oftentimes a rebate or additional discount will be available if you don't opt for the special rate. For instance, you can get 1 percent financing or an additional thousand-dollar rebate.

The reality is, you need to look at all the options to decide what's best for you, because many variables can be at play. This is best illustrated through concrete examples. Let's say you're financing $25,000, and you get the special financing rate of sixty months at .9 percent. That calculates to a $426.27 monthly payment. If you kept the loan for its entire term, you'd pay $576 in interest for a total cost of $25,576.

Now let's suppose that if you didn't take that special financing, there's a $1000 rebate. And then you could get 2.9% from your bank or another lender through the dealer. Now, you're only financing

$24,000 and your payment is $430 and interest then is $1800. So, in the end, you're paying $24,000 + $1,800 for a total of $25,800.

However, there's one instance where captive financing in this case would not be the more economical choice. If you think you might sell or trade in your car before the term of a loan ends, you're better off taking the rebate. The loan balance or payoff is higher for the subsidized rate loan all the way until the 49th payment. If you are someone who likes to trade in your car every two or three years, getting the rebate is the more financially sound choice.

Now that we've covered financing when purchasing, there is one other option you may also want to explore depending on your automobile needs and habits. The leasing option has become increasingly popular in recent years.

Twenty-five percent of all new cars are leased; almost half of all luxury cars are leased. In the major cities, such as Miami and New York, leasing rates can be as high as 80 percent.

The most obvious and alluring advantage of a lease is that you're not tied to the car for a long period. You will turn your car in at the end of a three-year term and get a shiny, new vehicle. This has become a more attractive option in recent years because of the exponentially rapid pace of advancements in technology. Such developments continue to increase at a record pace, leading consumers that don't want to be left behind and need the newest gadgets and safety features in their vehicle to consider nothing else but leasing.

Such developments can be a big selling point for a lot of people. Just last year was the first time that cars offered tight integration with your smart phone, with the phone screen popping up on your dash. No blind spot rear view mirrors and automatic steering technology are among many of the other recent offers with new leases.

Although you do not own the car during the lease, you always have the option with a leased vehicle to buy it out at the end of the residual value. The monthly payment is often lower on a lease and that's because you're only paying for the vehicle's depreciation during the lease term. So essentially, you're buying half a vehicle— at the end you can decide if you want to buy the other half. Only about 20 percent of consumers buy out in the end. The lease is often a very good deal because the manufacturers incentivize leases a lot more. They advertise lease payment terms to bring in new customers.

To summarize the benefits of a lease: You will not be stuck for a long period with the same vehicle. You will be getting a lower monthly payment than if you chose to purchase. In a lease, the leasing company has the risk of the future market value of the car, whereas if you buy *you* have the risk of the future market value. It's a crap shoot—no one knows for sure. It all depends on factors such as the robustness of the economy and the popularity of the model. Regardless, at the end of the three years you can walk away from the car. For example, suppose they guessed wrong about the depreciation—you can still walk away. If you bought the car three years into it and it's only worth $10,000 and not $12,500, you're $2,500 in the negative. If you know you want a new car in a few years, it's worthwhile to lease. If it's worth more than the lease estimation, you can always buy it and turn around and sell it for a profit on your own. Likewise, you can trade it in and get the additional equity in the car on a trade in. On the other hand, if they estimated an end of lease value that is higher than what the car is worth you can turn the car in and walk away, benefitting from their "mistake". Most of the time, the guess is high. Manufacturers often over-estimate the end value to get the lease payment down. For that reason, it makes even more sense to lease.

Even after deciding on a lease option, you need to work out the best terms for your needs. Some terms that may be helpful during such considerations are capitalized cost, rent charge and lease-end value.

The capitalized cost is the equivalent of the purchase price in a retail transaction. The question you want to ask regarding this should be, "If I lease, can I get a lower capitalized cost than if I buy the vehicle?" Sometimes the manufacturer offers additional rebates on a lease that aren't available on purchases.

Another important term in lease options is the rent charge, the equivalent of an interest rate on a financing option. It used to be that only people with good credit could get a lease, but that's changed significantly. Now there are lease terms offered for people with lower credit scores. The lease end value is also called the residual value—that's the calculated value of the vehicle at the end of the lease.

To calculate your monthly base payment before tax, simply add the capitalized cost, fees (such as license/registration), and the rent charge and divide by the number of months of the lease.

You will also want to consider how many miles you will drive. A standard lease usually allows 12,000 miles per year. If you drive more you can get a greater mileage allowance which will raise the monthly payment and lower the lease end value. Less miles will lower the monthly payment and raise the end value.

Whatever you decide to do regarding financing your new vehicle, realize that there are a range options available, so do your research and consider all options to make the best choice for your needs.

CHAPTER FIVE:

NEW OR USED

MOST PEOPLE THINK that when they are buying a used car that they are buying somebody else's problem, and this leads to even further anxiety. Some of this unease is warranted, as a used car has a history with one or more owners that you should know about and affects the value and function of the car. Thus, doing the research when buying a used car and establishing a relationship of trust with the seller or dealership is perhaps more important than when purchasing a new car.

This does not mean that such a venture need be feared, just that the same kind of preparation is needed as when buying a new a car...and then some.

First, let's look at the various options you have for buying a used car and the details involved with each option.

There are three major avenues you can pursue when purchasing a used a car. Let's review them—from the riskier propositions to the safer ones, which mirror buying a new car from a trusted dealership. When purchasing a used car, you basically have three options of purchase. You can buy from a private individual, an independent dealership that deals exclusively in used cars, or a new car dealership that is authorized to sell used cars that are known as "certified pre-owned" and other types of used cars that do not qualify under this definition. We will examine the advantages of buying a certified pre-owned car and the details involved when we get to this last option of purchase. First, however, let's look at the two other options and the relative advantages and drawbacks of each.

Many used car buyers decide to look for a used car sold by a private individual that owned the car before and now is looking to sell it. Such opportunities can be found listed in your local newspapers, through online used car sites, or on general classified sites such as Craigslist.

If you purchase from an individual – especially if they are the original owner – they most likely will be able to share extensive maintenance and repair history. Of course, a private seller may also leave out important information that would lower the ticket price of the car. It's up to you to decide how much you can trust the private seller.

Once you make an appointment to see the car, download a used car inspection checklist available from websites or magazines such as *Popular Mechanics*. This list guides you on important details to be examined in the car even before you take a test drive, including items to check on the car's exterior, the chassis, inside, and engine. In case you are not fully qualified to perform all these checklist items, you need to hire a mechanic to perform a checkup on any used car. Beware of any private seller who does not allow you to have your mechanic examine the car.

The second option when buying a used car is approaching an independent dealership that deals only in used cars.

You will find there are many advantages in buying a used car from a dealership. The dealership will complete all title and registration paperwork for you, avoiding the hassle of a trip to the DMV. The dealership can also serve as a one-stop shop for financing, extended warranty, and other protection policies. You can trade-in your car at a dealership and take advantage of the reduction in tax on your purchase as most states deduct the value of a trade for the taxable amount. Finally, you are more protected in purchasing from a dealer as there are stringent laws governing dealer operations, disclosures, and transactions.

This does not mean that the same precautions used when buying from a private seller necessarily should be overlooked. A dealership, however, has connections with companies such as Carfax and can provide interested customers with vehicle history reports of used cars. Such a history includes titling, accidents, and oftentimes service records. Most dealers offer copies of the report free of charge in-person or online. If you are buying from a private individual, you should consider ordering one to double-check and confirm information provided by the seller.

The third option is to buy a used car from a new car dealership. New car dealerships have an excellent source of well-maintained pre-owned vehicles through new car trade-ins and lease returns. New car dealers have fully equipped shops with trained and certified technicians and are therefore well-equipped to inspect, complete scheduled maintenance, and recondition used cars before they offer them for sale.

Cars of the same make as those sold by the brand dealership may be sold as certified pre-owned cars. Such programs are closely controlled by the factory manufacturers and the inspection of certified pre-owned vehicles is guided by a multi-point checklist that ensures the reconditioned car is in excellent condition to qualify as certified pre-owned. For instance, if the tires or the brakes do not meet the benchmarks of the checklist, they must be replaced. Only new car dealerships sell certified pre-owned cars, and as a used car buyer you are most protected with this option.

Certified pre-owned cars also come with a factory backed extended warranty that varies in length and coverage by manufacturer, and if you ever face a problem you can take it to any dealership service department of the same brand nationwide.

Some dealerships offer a return guarantee on used cars. That's a great indicator that you've chosen a dealership that goes out of its way to put the customer first.

Whatever option you settle on, make sure that you investigate the car's reconditioning history and that you get a full report from the seller. This will offer you a detailed history of any work done on the car after it was bought by the dealership, whether it was a new or a used car dealership. New car dealerships currently spend an average of $1,200 on reconditioning a used vehicle before offering it for sale. Used car dealerships spend a little less. Most states do not have any requirements on reconditioning, and used car dealerships usually do not have service departments so they must send cars out for reconditioning.

An important aspect of the vehicle's history to investigate closely when buying any type of used car is the accident history. Up to 30 percent of used cars have been involved in accidents that are serious enough to have been recorded in the vehicle history report obtained from agencies such as Carfax.

If an accident is reported it is usually rated minor, moderate, or severe. You should avoid cars that have been involved in severe accidents, because no matter how well they have been reconditioned, future problems may arise because of problems with the body or engine that could have been undetected. One of the most telling details that signal the severity of an accident is whether the air bags deployed during impact. If the air bags deployed, it was a serious accident no matter how it is listed in the accident report. As a rule, avoid any used cars with such a history.

Salvaged cars have been rebuilt from a damage of more than 50 percent of their original parts. Because such cars have been so drastically rebuilt, it is difficult to get the frame and other elements back to factory specifications. These cars are usually a lot cheaper, but clearly come with their own set of problems and risks.

Officially, in the car business, the term "lemon" refers to a new car that is re-purchased by the manufacturer from the consumer due to defects. The consumer then has the right to exchange the lemon for another vehicle. New car dealerships generally do not resell these lemons at all. Other used car dealerships, however, may buy the lemons at auctions and recondition them for sale as a used car. Such a history needs to be disclosed, and it is defined as a man-ufacture buyback on the title. If you are interested in buying one of these cars, have an independent mechanic perform a full checkup and give you a detailed report. As in other instances, if a seller does not allow this, consider this a serious red flag and move on to something else.

The last essential item to consider before driving your used car out of the lot is the type of service contract available so you are best protected in case problems arise. The buyer's guide will let you know of the type of warranty that each car still holds. All certified pre-owned cars come with a warranty, and they may have a new car warranty left on them. The Carfax vehicle history records any manufacturer warranty still available.

When purchasing a service-contract try to extend coverage to as long as you think you will own the car or at least the term of the loan. If financing, you can usually roll the cost of the service contract into your monthly payment. When protecting a new or recent model year car with a service contract it's best to consider the most comprehensive coverage as minor items such as replacing a window motor can be costly.

With an older car, full coverage might not make sense financially. With these cars, however, you should strongly consider a powertrain service contract that covers the car's major systems including the engine, transmission, and drivetrain.

Once you have decided on which path to pursue with the purchase of your used car, then, as with the new car purchase, it's time to make a deal. Being fully informed before going into the deal-making process is crucial. Let's examine the particulars of this more closely in the next chapter.

CHAPTER SIX:

LET'S MAKE A DEAL

THE TITLE OF THIS CHAPTER is a little misleading in that it implies that the deal-making portion of your purchase begins only at this level. While much of the details of the purchasing deal will be decided in consultation with the sales associate and the finance department during your visit to the dealership, the only way to make informed choices during each phase of the deal is to familiarize yourself with the terminology, the industry, and the process so that you can engage with the associate in a confident way and know which questions to ask.

As we have shown in the previous chapters, much of the work to ensure that you have the data needed at your mental disposal at this stage should be done in the weeks before this visit. In fact, one of the primary decisions arrived at from the preliminary research stage is the choice of a dealership and a sales associate with which you have established a comfortable and open connection. The more prepared and knowledgeable you are, the less stressful the give and take of the deal-making and the smoother the development of mutual trust.

As such, you should contact the sales associate with whom you previously established a connection during your research to set up an appointment to visit the dealership. This associate will not only be familiar with the general details of your situation but may have already set up a potential client file with information you provided and can offer valuable insights on specific issues you feel are most important, thus saving you energy and time. There are also situations in which you may want to address more specific questions with the associate, such as when checking to make sure an advertised pre-owned car is currently available.

The associate also serves as your guide into other departments such as finance and service, as well as introducing you perhaps to the owners or managers of the dealership or other sales associates so that you feel welcome as part of the larger family. Depending on the specifics of your search, the associate can conduct preliminary steps before you come in for your visit, such as compiling a vehicle history, Carfax report, and trim packages. Ask the associate to conduct other important tasks that you want accomplished before you visit the dealership.

By this point, the sales associate has made it a mission to make sure that all your concerns are addressed as thoroughly as possible so that you make your planned visit and follow through with the purchase, so don't be shy about exploiting the associate's expertise and access to crucial data that is sometimes only available to dealerships.

By all means, if you have narrowed down your choices after taking advantage of such expertise, take a test drive. The time you spend in your car will almost exclusively be behind the wheel driving it. It seems absurd not to see what that feels like before you commit so much money to its purchase.

A test drive will provide you with crucial information about the automobile that you cannot acquire any other way, no matter how helpful the sales associate or how thorough your research. Only getting your hands physically on the wheel will let you know if it is too tight, too loose, or just right for your personal preference. If the response is tight it means it responds very quickly. Looser is safer and more comfortable for highway driving. Speaking of which, make sure a stretch of the test drive is on a highway to evaluate performance at these speeds.

If you are planning on trading in an old car, bring in any service or repair history with you on the visit. This will help the dealer make a more informed estimate of the value of the trade-in. For instance, if you recently had new tires installed, this can significantly affect the final figure. Also, tidy up the car, clean it, and empty it out of all personal property and other materials. The trade-in doesn't have to be spotless, but make sure it's clutter free to ensure a quick evaluation. Do some research on your own to get a couple of values on pricing from sources such as *Kelley Blue Book*. You want to make sure that the trade-in price you accept is in the general ballpark of a car in similar condition.

Car valuation is based on a few measures, including the state of the current market, the condition of the car, and its history. The dealer usually makes an offer on the spot after an inspection and test drive of the trade-in. The sales manager then approves the offer. Dealers are happy with doing research beforehand if requested.

They look at wholesale transactions of car auction data within the past week or so for similar vehicles, and this helps them make a more precise evaluation.

Most dealers will take almost any car as trade-in no matter what the condition as a service to the customer. Don't feel as if you must give them a trade-in that is immediately ready to be resold as a used car on the spot. Almost all trade-ins require some reconditioning before they can be resold. Cars that have been salvaged or are in very poor condition retain some value for their parts and, of course, fetch a lower trade-in price.

Before you make the decision on whether to trade in your car at the dealership or sell it yourself you should closely consider a few variables beyond the opportunity to get a higher price in the open market. From advertising the sale to showing the car to prospective buyers to making sure the title and all financial carryovers are properly transferred, selling a car can be a time-consuming and sometimes complex procedure. In most states, you also get a tax credit for trading in your old car, whereas the portion of the sticker price covered by the funds from a private sale is taxed regularly when you purchase a new car.

After you have taken care of trade-in deduction if applicable, lay the groundwork to get the best possible package on the new or used model you want. Most dealers have already discounted the price from the manufacturer suggested retail price (MSRP). This sale price is the one that commonly appears in ads, so you want to make sure that you begin your planning with that number in mind. Thin profit margins on these sales make it almost impossible for the dealer to offer anything much below the sale price.

The profit margin in the car industry has decreased steadily in recent years. On the sale of new cars, the gross profit margin hovers at around 3.5 percent. On used car sales, it is a bit higher at 12 percent. However, this is before the dealership covers any expenses for running the business, such as personnel salary and dealership maintenance. Net profit for new car sales is negative, and even the used car sales department breaks about even. The significant net profit in most dealerships comes mostly from service. Financing can be somewhat profitable if they sell enough extended coverage. From the customer's perspective, this is to say that the focus of making a deal should be less on haggling to slash the sticker price, for which there may not be any bargaining room, and more on getting the best full package including trade-in price, rebate, service contract, and financing.

Once you find a trusted dealer, and you're confident overall with the sticker price below the MSRP, you have completed a big part of the deal. This does not necessarily mean that you should curtail your proactive participation in the sales process at this point and disengage. Although the dealer cannot discount much lower than the sale price because of narrow profit margins, other possibilities exist for deal-making, such as factory rebates and financing or leasing options, programs whose costs are covered completely by the manufacturer.

Have the salesperson break down the price for you. Ask if there are bigger discounts available for certain types of finance or leasing programs.

After you have exhausted the associate's knowledge of all the options available and how this affects your monthly budget depending on the payments and your overall budget depending on the total cost, you can evaluate the range of choices and confidently begin to close the deal. It may be that the final deal meets all your original expectations, or more likely it may be that you became more knowledgeable about certain aspects of this last stage of the purchase experience and you had to adjust your expectations to best suit your current needs and means.

If it has been a while since you last purchased a car, your final decision may have been influenced by recent trends in car owner-ship that have changed many aspects of how dealerships strive to keep customers happy and satisfied in the long range.

Such innovations have always been part of the automotive sales industry and are designed to fulfill the primary objective of any successful dealership: to make sure that the customer drives away from the lot knowing that they got the best car for the best value and one that was best suited to the current situation, financial and otherwise. The best dealerships know that this is the best way to ensure customer loyalty and the invaluable benefits reaped from such intangibles as word-of-mouth praise.

Dealerships need to meet their end of the bargain in offering a wide variety of buying options and services to ensure customer satisfaction and ideally life-long loyalty, but a well-prepared and confident customer also helps to make the relationship trustworthy and ensures that both sides benefit from the deal in the long term.

Preparation is confidence that builds trust. This truism is as valid today in the car sales industry as it was in the days when my grand-father Sam opened his first used car dealership on Newark Avenue. Customers back then did not have the kind of access to information that customers do today, but Sam applied the same principles that his father applied for success of the bakery—one of them was that expertise in customer needs and wants was as important as quality in the service and excellence in the product sold.

Back then, the customer's education in the process of purchas-ing a car and keeping it in good condition through regular servicing and tune ups took place in the interactions and exchanges of information with dealership owners like Sam and his service and sales team. In time, this made for a savvier customer base that created a demand for more in depth information about the car industry and critical reviews of its products. With the ascent of the Internet, such information previously limited to specialty magazines and professional journals became more readily available.

Today's car dealership associates expect to deal with a sophisticated customer that not only has researched the specific type of car desired but is in general more educated about the industry and its products so will naturally be more confident in the queries presented and impatient with canned responses. The educated consumer is a boon to any industry because it challenges businesses to meet higher levels of expectations.

CHAPTER SEVEN:

RETHINKING "THE BOX"
AND OTHER UPDATES

BACK IN THE DAYS BEFORE REGULATIONS, after customers had selected a car from the lot and negotiated a price they stepped into the ring of the finance office which was known in the industry vernacular as "the box." This is where the innocent customers lost all hope of surviving the sleazy tactics of De Niro like "box men" intent on hoodwinking them. As discussed earlier, such stereotypes have some basis in earlier times, and are certainly antithetical to the customer-centric ethos that is more commonplace in quality dealerships today.

This does not mean that there are not negotiations made and deals sealed in "the box" these days, but that the atmosphere can be much less antagonistic. A customer still should know the ropes and be prepared to evaluate finance or lease options, insurance and maintenance plans, and service contract levels. As opposed to seeing this step as a final showdown, in a well-chosen dealership sealing the deal in the finance office or business office can be an opportunity to accurately review the details of this important transaction and begin your ownership experience on a great footing.

From your very first contact at the dealership, a sales associate should be asking you questions and gathering information about what you want, how that dovetails with your financial situation, how much research you have completed, and what issues remain unresolved. A good salesperson becomes a partner in your quest and not some challenge to overcome. The value of an effective salesperson is the expertise that can be deployed on the buyer's behalf to make sure the buyer is satisfied. Under ideal circumstances a salesperson's expertise sharpens and fine tunes the knowledge the buyer has gained from their initial research.

In general, as with other areas of life, be wary of any offer that sounds too good to be true. Such sales tactics may help dealers sell more cars in the short run but it undermines the trust necessary to build a return-customer base or the long term. Read the fine print on the advertising, and heed clever phrasing, such as a price advertised with fine-print tagged on it such as "plus $2,000 cash down."

The good news is that if you do your research ahead of time you expand your range of choices by educating yourself on previously unknown options. You have also become an engaged consumer and thus are more apt to consider options that may be even better suited to your needs than your original one. You are also not likely to be intimidated by a sales associate that does not have to guess at your desires from vague and uninformed bits of information. You know what the dealership *should* be doing and what the sales associate *should* be saying at this stage to confirm that you're making a wise decision.

When you are working with your sales consultant, get an introduction to the service department as that can and should influence your choice of dealership. While the service department has not featured much in what attracts the customer to the dealership in the pre-buying and buying stages, the savvy consumer has done some research on post-purchase customer and vehicle service even if just reading up on the company's website or perusing customer reviews. On the initial visits, customers should be made fully aware of all aspects of this versatile and important department in a dealership. New car dealerships have service departments with the latest tools and a staff of technicians that receive regular technical training.

The service department plays a crucial role in maintaining your new investment. In some ways, you are choosing a home for your car and a team that will help you maintain your new purchase and keep it functioning at its optimal level long after all the warranties have expired. If a customer is satisfied with the purchase, but particularly with the service provided throughout the life of the car, the next time that customer is in the market for a car, the natural place to start is the dealership that such a customer now considers family and has proven to deliver not only a quality product but support for that product throughout.

In this sense, the ideal ending for this process as set out in the early pages of this guide may also need to be adjusted and rethought in this closing section. A dealership owner should not be complacent with you driving away beaming over a deal for the highest quality automobile, the exact model you wanted, at the best value. As such a member of the dealership family, you would be in your infancy and must be nurtured as such from the very moment of your first return trip to the service department. It may have been the price on a vehicle that attracted you and the flexible financing that closed the deal, but it is the care and attention lavished on you and your vehicle post-sale that will ensure you become a lifetime client.

JOE DIFEO grew up in Northeast New Jersey where the DiFeo name has been synonymous with cars and customer service from the 40's on due to his grandfather Sam's philosophy that "good business is about relationships, not transactions."

Joe currently owns and operates Volkswagen of Saint Augustine in Northeast Florida. He helps a team of thirty plus A players serve customers guided by his grandfather's philosophy and core values that come from the H.E.A.R.T – Helpful, Efficient, Always Improving, Respectful, and Thankful.

When he's not at the dealership he plays piano, guitar, and mandolin every chance he gets and enjoys the outdoors with his wife Sway and twin children Charlie and Sophia.

He'd love to hear from you at joedifeo@vwsaintaug.com

Made in the USA
Middletown, DE
24 June 2018